Every summer Bobbie, Harper and I go to scout camp together. I was really excited this year, because we're all in the same cabin. But then a new scout called Taylor turned up to stay with us.

Taylor makes jokes and acts cool. But Taylor's jokes aren't always funny. Sometimes they're mean.

3

Yesterday I told Taylor I wash cars for money to pay for camp. Taylor told everyone at our lunch table I had to wash cars because I'm poor.

Some of the other children giggled. I felt my cheeks turn bright red. I left the table.

"Only joking!" Taylor called after me, laughing.

After dinner Taylor pulled Bobbie and Harper aside and whispered something to them. Soon they headed my way.

"Jamie, Taylor is going to buy us all ice creams," said Harper. **"Want to come?"**

"Actually, I don't have enough money for four cones," said Taylor. **"So if you want to come, Jamie, you'll have to pay for your own."**

Taylor paused for a second. **"Oh, but you probably can't afford ice cream because you're poor."** Taylor shrugged. **"Sorry!"**

6

The three of them left, and I was alone.

A person doesn't need to hit or call someone names to be a bully. Sometimes a bully will leave someone out of an activity on purpose. He or she will also encourage others in the group to exclude the person.

Later, Bobbie, Harper and Taylor walked into the cabin with their ice creams. They were whispering and laughing.

I was trying to read, but I felt ashamed and angry. Bobbie and Harper are *my* friends. Why was Taylor picking on me?

The three sat on Taylor's bunk. **"Jamie, come and join us!"** Bobbie called.

"Yeah, Jamie," said Taylor. **"Come and tell us more stories about being poor."**

I turned towards the wall, pretending to read. Then I started to cry. I couldn't help it.

"I was only joking!" sighed Taylor. **"Learn how to take a joke."**

Sometimes jokes can be fun. But they can go too far. If jokes or teasing make you feel upset or angry, it's OK to tell the other person to stop.

Today we're writing postcards to our parents.
But Bobbie, Harper and Taylor are laughing and
whispering instead of writing.

Suddenly they go very quiet. I look over and see Harper
give me a dirty look. Bobbie looks ready to cry. Taylor is
smirking. I ask Harper and Bobbie what's wrong, but they
both ignore me.

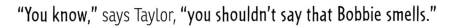

"You know," says Taylor, "you shouldn't say that Bobbie smells."

The three of them get up and walk away before I can say anything.
I didn't say that Bobbie smelled!

Some bullies will gossip or spread rumours. By telling lies or embarrassing stories, they can get other children to dislike or bully the person too.

Tonight at the campfire, Harper and Bobbie pretend I'm not here. I'm sitting right next to them!

They talk about the big fishing trip we are going on at the end of the week.

"We're staying in three-person tents," says Taylor. "You and Bobbie will stay with me." Harper nods in agreement.

"But what about Jamie?" I hear Bobbie whisper to Harper.

Taylor's eyes roll. "Come on, Bobbie," Taylor says. "You don't want to be friends with someone who says mean things about you."

"Mean things?" I ask loudly. "I didn't say you smelled, Bobbie!"

They still pretend I'm not here. I feel so upset and frustrated. I give up and leave.

In the morning, I sit by myself at breakfast. I find an empty table at lunchtime too.

I feel so alone.

Back at my cabin, I see a group of children gathered around the front door. When they see me, some of them giggle. Others walk away with their heads down.

There on the door is a photo of me when I was younger. I'm holding my favourite teddy and sucking my thumb. Someone has written **"baby bed wetter"** on the photo.

I run away from the cabin as fast as I can.

·CABIN 4·

BABY BED WETTER

Bobbie finds me. **"What do you want?"** I mumble.

"I want to say I'm sorry," says Bobbie. **"I should have stood up for you. I wasn't being a good friend. I was afraid if I did, Taylor would make fun of me too."**

"I didn't say you smelled," I say. **"I would never say mean things about you."**

"I know that now," says Bobbie, smiling sadly.

People who watch bullying happening are called bystanders. Bystanders can help to stop bullying by sticking up for others. If you see someone being bullied, tell the bully to stop or ask an adult for help.

Bobbie and I walk back towards the cabins. We're surprised to see Harper shouting at Taylor.

"I can't believe you stole that photo from me!" Harper yells. "I should never have shown it to you."

"Calm down!" Taylor laughs. "It was just a joke."

"Sometimes your jokes aren't funny, Taylor. Sometimes they're just mean!" Haper says.

Harper walks over to us. "I'm really sorry about the photo, Jamie," Harper says. "I hope we can still be friends."

Harper thinks we should talk to an adult about what Taylor has said and done. We tell our scout leader, Alex, about how mean Taylor has been. Alex listens to us.

"I'm glad you came to me," Alex says. "Joking around with friends can be fun. But sometimes joking goes too far, and friends get hurt. Some people use jokes as an excuse to say hurtful things, and that's not OK. Mean jokes and spreading rumours to hurt or embarrass someone is bullying."

I hadn't thought of it that way. But it makes sense. I feel a lot better after talking to Alex.

It's good to stand up for yourself and others. But you shouldn't try to handle bullying alone. It's always best to tell an adult you trust. The adult can stop the bullying behaviour and get everyone the help he or she needs.

Alex moves Taylor to a different cabin. I don't see Taylor much after that, which is fine with me. Bobbie and Harper stay away from Taylor too.

As punishment for bullying, Taylor isn't allowed to go on the fishing trip. Bobbie, Harper and I have a great time.

It wasn't the perfect summer, but the end of scout camp was fun. And we all learned a good lesson. Sometimes jokes aren't funny.